D0661396

HELPS
FOR THE
SCRUPULOUS

Russell M. Abata, C.SS.R., S.T.D.

LIGUORI
PUBLICATIONS

One Liguori Drive
Liguori, Mo. 63057
(314) 464-2500

Imprimi Potest:
Edmund T. Langton, C.SS.R.
Provincial, St. Louis Province
The Redemptorists

Imprimatur:
+ Charles R. Koester
Vicar General of St. Louis

ISBN 0-89243-061-3
Library of Congress Catalog Card Number: 76-21430

To all those who suffer scruples and have not found the understanding they need nor the peace they desire.

TABLE OF CONTENTS

INTRODUCTION

This book is intended for people who have become paralyzed by a fear of sin. Their main worry is over serious sin and its threatened punishment of hell, but in their panic such persons react excessively to all sin, and even to what might look like sin.

Because of the excessive precautions they take in dealing with sin, such persons are called "scrupulous."

Sin haunts them.

They are haunted by past sins. They are haunted with present temptations and decisions. They are haunted about their future and what is to become of them. No amount of reassurance seems capable of setting them at ease.

Who are these people?

They come from every walk of life — young and old, married and single, rich and poor, highly and normally educated. It does not seem to matter. They are all terrified of sin and this terror, more or less, has had a devastating effect on their lives.

To offer some guidelines for relief from this terror is the purpose of this book.

"But," you might wonder, "if personal attention cannot calm this terror, what can a book hope to accomplish?"

This is a fair question.

First, some scrupulous people do not realize they have a need for specialized help. A book can help them recognize this need.

Second, a book can act as a reminder. So often scrupulous persons do not remember the words of their counselor. His words seemed clear enough — until the scrupulous person is alone with his fears. Then he forgets everything. A book can be a printed, enduring echo of the counselor's spoken words.

It is hoped that this book will be like a first aid kit. It should be kept handy and consulted as needed.

CHAPTER 1

Are You Scrupulous?

No one wants to be given a label, especially if it sounds bad.

To label packaged or canned goods to tell us what is inside without having to open them is helpful.

But to label a human being is not. It can even be unfair. Once people see or hear a label, they tend to stop looking or listening. They feel they know all they want to know about that person.

It is so with the label or name, "scrupulous."

Once a person is considered scrupulous, he is separated from others. Members of his family look on him with sadness, and even disgust. They apologize to their friends for his conduct. They are not sure what it is all about, but they know it is bad. Strangers laugh at him and his worries. Everyone, even priests, suddenly seems to be busy or in a hurry when he appears.

These unfavorable reactions are enough to make many not want to face the fact that they are scrupulous, and that they are different from others who are considered normal.

Facing the Real Problem

But trying to hide such a condition from one's self and others is not wise.

It is bound to show.

More important, it is a condition that needs to be acknowledged and attended to as early as possible. No human being should have to put up with such agony.

Furthermore, if the person himself does not realistically face his condition and what is really causing it, he could exhaust himself on solving lesser problems and completely over-look the real problem.

For example, so many scrupulous people wrongly place all the blame for their upsetment on their inability to make an exact confession of their sins.

Others blame their lack of feelings. They are afraid their sins have not been forgiven. Why? Because they do not feel forgiven. They *say* they are sorry for their sins, but they do not *feel* sorry; so how can they be sure they are forgiven?

Others blame sex. If they could only eliminate sexual feelings, they believe they would be alright.

Still others put the blame on all the life situations that gang up on them. If life would not hit them with so many problems, they feel they would be O.K. As it is, they just cannot catch up with it all.

Without a doubt, each of these problems complicates the scrupulous person's life, but his biggest problem is fear. He is deathly afraid of pain.

The Fear of Hell

The pain that terrifies and sends the scrupulous person into panic is the possibility of going to hell.

Somewhere inside of him are the screams and warnings of teachers and preachers about the fire and burning, snakes and rats, thirst and hunger, rejection, loneliness, and pains that await him if he dies in mortal sin. And it will never, never, never end.

He decided a long time ago that hell is one place he does not want to go.

Although he has often blocked off his fear of hell and carelessly gone off in search of pleasures of every kind, this fear of hell has never died.

Now, for real or for imagined reasons he finds himself faced with the possibility of going to hell. Whatever he has done — made a bad Confession, stolen money from a church, lived a life of sexual abuse — he is afraid he cannot straighten it out and make things right with God.

"I am scared."

"What are you scared of?"

"I am scared of all my sins. I am scared that God will not forgive me. I have been so bad."

"But why will God not forgive you?"

"I don't know. I can't explain it. I just do not feel that he will. No matter what I do, I just can't make things right. I'm afraid God is going to punish me severely."

Many Roads but One Driver

So, regardless of why the fear of going to hell has become so real to him, the scrupulous person is in panic. It consumes him. He cannot rest until he has stomped out any sin that could send him to hell. He rushes back to past actions to recheck them. He tears apart present actions to make sure of them. He leaps to future actions and how he is going to avoid sinning. He is suspicious of everything and accuses even the most innocent actions of sin. There was something wrong with the action or his intentions or the way he did it or something.

There is no reasoning with his panic.

One cannot even use other fears, such as the harm he is doing to his health or the hurt he is causing others, to stop the exaggerated and wrong judgments he is making.

Like a frightened child before an accusing, angry parent, he blurts out, "I did it. I did it. I am guilty. I'll confess to anything."

It is a desperate confession that hopes to silence the accusing voices of panic he hears inside his head. "For fear that I might have done it, I'll confess that I did. To play it safe, I'll confess that it was a serious sin."

Unfortunately, after a while, he has accused himself of so many serious sins that he has backed himself into a corner. He can hardly make a move until he has been reassured many times over that it is alright.

If the Description Fits

If you are terrorized by sin, you are scrupulous.

If sin is all you can think of, you are scrupulous.

If panic has you accusing yourself of serious sin on very little evidence, you are scrupulous.

You are not the greatest sinner alive.

You are not the greatest saint.

You are simply a person with a serious problem.

But how can you be sure you are judging your life and actions too severely?

This could present a problem. In your fearful state, it might be impossible for you to make such a judgment.

This is understandable. You know you. You know how you like the easy, lazy way out of problems. Claiming to be scrupulous might seem like you are making excuses and seeking an easy way out.

And yet, it is important for you to be honest about your condition. Otherwise, you will neither see nor be able to correct what is really wrong.

So, if you cannot make this judgment about yourself, then ask someone who is an expert in such matters to help you. Also, the examples given in Chapter Two of this book might help you reach your decision.

Either way, it is important for you to start with the fact that you are scrupulous. That, at least, is a beginning. This book and a good counselor can help you go from there to treat your problem.

A Word of Comfort

How many times you have wanted to despair and give up your struggle, but you did not.

This is to your credit.

God knows how hard you have struggled. And it all counts. None of it is wasted. It might seem like a waste, but in God's eyes and ways your efforts have a value.

In a human way, you need help and you must help yourself. You need a steady diet of understanding and solid advice.

You need to be freed of your panic.

This freedom can be accomplished, but it cannot be accomplished all at once. You need some correct knowledge of what exactly is expected of you. Your "play-it-safe" way of acting only gives in to your panic. You also need to take some shortcuts to be freed from the past and be able to concentrate on the present moment. And most of all, you need a workable escape hatch when panic strikes.

This book hopes to give you the necessary knowledge, some important shortcuts, and a workable escape hatch. On your part, you will have to give your best efforts and patience in learning and applying these helps.

In a few words, freedom can be yours, but you will have to do your part to acquire it.

CHAPTER 2
Is One of These You ?

Although scrupulous people find a number of areas, of life too fearful to handle, the following five are the worst — sex, anger, stealing, Confession, and a purpose of amendment.

The lives of Bruce, Jean, Timothy, Ann, and Michael will point out some of the difficulties of these areas.

Bruce

Bruce is preoccupied with the sins he has committed and those he might commit.

Bruce was his mother's favorite. In front of her, he was an angel. Away from her, he was someone else.

When Bruce was old enough to experience sex, it became the driving force of his life. He sought it everywhere — inside and outside of marriage.

This went on for years.

Then a day of reckoning came. Bruce was beginning to take death and final judgment seriously. Looking back over his life, he really became frightened. There was so much to account for.

Again and again he went to Confession. It never seemed enough.

Finally, his worry and concentration shifted from the past to the present. He was obsessed with the fear of sinning. Every girl — whether old or young, in person or on TV or in a magazine, on the street or in church — every girl became a source of danger.

He simply did not know what to do. He could

not keep his mind blank of everything sexual. Something was bound to catch him off-guard. When it did, he was terrified that he might yield to the pleasures he felt.

Bruce began to retreat more and more from women, away from reality.

He was backing himself into himself, and all he could feel was panic.

Bruce was so scared of his sexual feelings that he begged God and his pure Mother to free him of all such feelings. He wore the rosary around his neck and carried dozens of holy pictures to obtain this favor from God. But again and again sexual feelings broke through and he felt God had let him down.

Bruce needs specialized help.

Jean

Jean is over-worried about harming and even killing people.

In order to avoid the slightest possibility of harming anyone, she constantly washes her hands when cooking. She rechecks the gas several times to make sure it is off. If a bubble is left on a dish she has washed and rinsed, she rinses all of them over again —just to be sure it was not a soap bubble.

These are only a few of the safeguards Jean uses to make sure she has not hurt anyone.

To look at Jean, you would never suspect that a fear of killing people could be a problem.

Jean is a lady.

She was taught from early childhood not to feel or display anger, not even a tantrum.

Proper little ladies did not do such things.

As Jean grew she found a way to avoid anger. She simply avoided angry people and anger-producing situations. Besides, her ready smile and willingness to help others made almost everyone her friend.

But as she grew older and took on the responsibilities of marriage and motherhood, Jean began to experience a growing uneasiness. Strange thoughts of harming people crossed her mind. She was horrified. Why was she feeling this way? Could she have harmed someone without realizing it and now her conscience was bothering her?

Jean did not know.

She only knew she was too scared to take any chances with danger, even the slightest danger. Left to her imagination and panic, she would magnify any danger into a catastrophe. So she has to be supercautious to avoid all danger.

Unfortunately, Jean's fear of harming others did not stay in the areas where she might be doing the physical harm herself. It also went over into the area where she feared she was calling evil or giving others over to the devil. This sent her panic up even higher.

If you were to slow down Jean's racing mind and ask her, "Do you really think you have harmed anyone?" she would answer, "I do not *think* I have hurt anyone, and yet, I *feel* I might have."

She is not sure.

It is this not being sure that scares Jean. She is constantly pleading with people in authority to reassure her that she has not hurt anyone.

Timothy

Timothy is retired.

Not having the pressures of his job any longer — and the long trip back and forth each day — Timothy has a lot of time on his hands. He has a lot of time for thinking and for worrying.

As Timothy sits alone with his newspaper, he reads about investigations to catch those who have been cheating on taxes, collecting unemployment while working a secret, side job, of doctor's overcharging for services because some health plan or the government would pay it, etc. The more he reads, the more upset Timothy gets. In one form or other, Timothy has done these things or been a party to such dealings.

Even worse than such dishonesty, he has cheated by sleeping on the job, taking off early, not working as hard as he could have, and taking things home that did not belong to him. He worried somewhat at the time, but somehow he or others convinced him not to worry about such things. Everybody was doing it. So, he went along with it.

But now Timothy is worried, really worried. What is he to do? Must he turn himself in? Must he pay all that money back? What will his family think of him if he does?

What is Timothy to do? To do nothing is bad. To do something is equally bad. He is stuck. "And to think that I was looking forward to retirement!" he moans. "What is to become of me?"

Ann

Ann is an elderly woman whose life has been wasted by her worries over Confession. The mere thought of Confession is so horrible that it starts her head and body shaking.

How did all of this begin?

It began at the age of fifteen, the first time Ann touched herself impurely.

While she was absorbed in her first experience with sexual pleasure, Ann only vaguely felt guilty. But after the experience was over, she was shocked over what she had done. She had never felt so degraded.

Ann tried to put the experience out of her mind, but no distraction could completely absorb her. By Saturday of that week, she knew she had to go to Confession.

The hours before she entered the confessional seemed to hurry and to drag. When she thought of the shame of telling another what she had done, she wanted to put it off. When she felt the pressure of guilt, she wanted to hurry and get it over.

Ann entered the confessional in a state of semi-shock.

She started her Confession with her less shameful sins. Then came the big one. She blurted out that she had impure thoughts. She could not force herself to mention that she had impure actions.

Soon Ann was out of the confessional, and her fear of confessing began. She knew she would never be able to bring herself to admit that shameful sin. Besides, she now added a sacrilege to her guilt. Both sins would make going to Confession a lifelong torture.

Michael

Michael, a man in his thirties, worries about his purpose of amendment.

How can he convince himself that he will not sin again when he knows he will? To say that he will "try" not to sin again seems like a lie or a game.

Michael — knowing himself pretty well — has good reasons to doubt the sincerity of his efforts not to sin again.

He lives to get pleasure and to avoid pain. He uses all of his energies for this purpose. How can he be sure, then, that he can resist a sinful pleasure? As a matter of fact, his record would seem to indicate that he cannot.

Because he is run by this pleasure-pain way of acting, Michael knows that his only hope of resisting sinful pleasures is to keep the pain of punishment ever before his eyes. It is this fear of punishment that prompts his sorrow for sin and hopefully can give him a purpose of amendment.

Can Michael be sure that he can keep the pain of punishment ever before his eyes? He doubts that he can.

At the moment he has had a good scare with death and so he is determined not to sin, but when the scare passes, he fears that he will return to his old ways of acting.

So, how can he be sure that he has a good enough purpose of amendment to take away his sins? This is Michael's torture.

You

Do you find a reflection of yourself in any of these five persons?

If you do, you will find a detailed treatment of each in later chapters. Each person will be given a complete chapter.

If you do not find yourself in any of these persons, then perhaps the chapters that follow immediately will touch on your particular condition and problems.

CHAPTER 3

Where Scruples Enter

If you take a good look at yourself, you will find that there are two sides to you.

There is an easygoing side and a worrying side.

Whereas your easygoing side does not want you to get upset over anything, your worrying side never lets up in finding fault with you. So often, like a tug of war inside of your head, each side has tried to pull you over to its way of looking at life.

But now, because you are really scared, the worrying side of you has taken over control. It has you taking everything so seriously that you are constantly upset. Your easygoing side hardly exists.

It is the complete taking over of your worrying side that is making you "scrupulous."

We will use this chapter to examine both of these sides of your personality. If you can see these two sides at work, you will have come a long way in understanding what has happened to you. This is the first step in understanding your condition.

The Easygoing Side

On the easygoing side, you want *what* you want, *when* you want it, and you cannot understand why you cannot have it, especially if it is not going to hurt anyone.

In regard to people, you want them available to help you but not to impose on you or take away your freedom.

In regard to life, you want to be always happy. If something goes wrong and you are faced with unhappiness, you become confused and upset. This is not the way it was supposed to turn out. Besides you might feel that you have already had too much suffering and disappointment from life. You feel cheated.

So, on the easygoing side of you, you feel that you should neither be denied any of the nice things you like nor forced to accept any of the painful things you do not like.

In a few words, this side of you has you always on the lookout to get as much pleasure and to avoid as much pain as is possible. If there is any pleasure to be had, you want it. If there is any pain facing you, you try your best to dodge it.

Actually, this intense seeking for pleasure and avoiding of pain is the child side of you.

The Worrying Side

Almost the opposite of this easygoing side, you also have a worrying side that is very hard on you. It never seems pleased with anything you do and has you always on edge over something.

Why is this worrying side so hard on you?

It acts this way to keep you out of trouble. It knows how carefree and careless your easygoing side can make you. It acts like a conscience to warn you of danger.

But, unfortunately, this worrying side of you can go overboard and have you feel guilty over almost anything. Like an inspecting army officer looking for faults, it can have you examine and re-examine the smallest details of your actions. It is not satisfied until they look

27

100 percent right.

Actually, the warnings that your worrying side uses to frighten you are pretty much an echo of the warnings you heard from your parents, teachers, and preachers. So often their message was, "You are not good enough. You should have done better. Now you have to worry about being scolded and punished." Somehow you got the impression that they — and God — would only be satisfied when your actions were as good, pure, and unselfish as the saints they held up as examples. If your actions were not, you had to worry until they were.

A Hindrance or a Help?

Having these two sides to your personality can be a hindrance. Your worrying side is constantly battling your easygoing side. Your worrying side argues, "You must do this. You are guilty over that." Your easygoing side answers, "I do not have to do it. I am not guilty."

If out of fear, fatigue, or a headache, your easygoing side always gives in to your worrying side, just to stop the arguing or to play it safe, you have a fully developed case of scruples on your hands. You have become a victim of your worrying side.

Regrettably, your quick plea of "I am guilty" does not stop your panic or the arguing in your head because now there arises the arguing over how to handle the guilt. Once again, for the sake of some kind of peace, your easygoing side gives in to your worrying side, even to the point of being ridiculous.

But, having these two sides to your personality does not have to be a hindrance. They can be helpful to give you a fuller picture of life. While your worrying side gives you a serious point of view, your easygoing side gives you a relaxed point of view. It is up to you to decide which is better to follow in each action. At times, you will follow your worrying side. At times, you will follow your easygoing side. At other times, you will follow some middle path — not too serious, not too lax.

Not Just One Side

So you are "scrupulous" because your worrying side is in complete control of you and is forcing you to be overcautious in everything that in any way looks like sin. There is no letup.

Obviously, such an overserious approach to life is unhealthy and wrong. You need some kind of balance.

So, if you have lost or have never found the easygoing side of you, it must be found. Even in something as important as making things right with God, a sense of humor and some good laughter can be as important to you as prayer.

"But," you might say, "I feel that I have been so bad that I have a right to be worried. I cannot see anything funny in anything. I am scared, really scared, and this might be my last chance to make things right with God. I cannot take any more chances. I have to listen and do what my worrying side says — not just to quiet it but because what it says is right."

Your fear is understandable. And *if* what you have done is wrong, you cannot wipe it away with a nervous laugh. It is wrong and must be taken care of sensibly. This does not mean becoming so frightened that everything inside of you becomes as unreasonable as a stampeding crowd in a burning building. Taking care of it that way is not going to make you feel better. It is not going to take away your panic.

"But," you might continue, "if I do not panic and take things so seriously, I will let up and before you know it my easygoing side will have me in trouble again. If I do not keep a constant pressure on myself, I'll become lazy, careless, selfish, and even sinful. So, I cannot let up for a moment. And even though you mean well in telling me to let up, you are only making it more difficult for me to control my easygoing side. To let up is to lose control."

Making Sense, but . . .

Without a doubt, you are making a lot of sense in what you are saying. It would be foolish to take control away from your worrying side and let your easygoing side take over. Your situation would become as bad, and perhaps even worse, than it is now.

No, neither your worrying side nor your easygoing side should be given the control over you. As we will consider in Chapter Six, only *you,* your personality, should have control over you — not a side or part of you.

For the present, it is enough for you to realize that listening to and following only your worrying side is not wise. It accomplishes nothing to worry yourself sick. Besides, such a one-sided, severe approach to life is not a guarantee that you are doing what God wants of you. It might be what your fears and the fears of those who trained you want, but not necessarily God.

In our next chapter, we will try to clear up what God really wants of you. Seeing some of the differences between what God wants and what your worrying side wants, you will be in a better position to realize how excessive the demands of your worrying side are. And, although seeing the truth and accepting the truth are not the same, it can be a start away from the control your worrying side has over you.

CHAPTER 4

God or You as Judge and Punisher?

The reason for the nightmare you are living is your fear of God's punishment.

Rightly or wrongly, you are so scared of being punished that you cannot feel safe or relaxed for a moment. You feel that the only hope you have to escape God's punishment is to completely stay away from everything that in any way looks like sin. This way you will keep at a safe distance from anything that really is sinful and you will convince God how sincerely sorry you are for what you have done and that you really are trying not to sin again.

Despite how scared you are over what you have been and how necessary it might seem to you to be hard on yourself to keep you away from sin, you are taking the wrong road. You are demanding more of yourself than God is.

Thus, while God only asks that you make a reasonable effort to keep his law, you are insisting on unreasonable, panic precautions.

Also, with God there would be some element of mercy based on your condition. With you, there is no mercy. Everything is being measured in terms of the strictest justice. You are not taking any chances of leaving your safety to another. Besides, you know you. You are afraid that mercy is just the excuse your easygoing side would use to get away with things.

Obviously, in a choice between God's ways of judging and punishing and your ways, God's ways are to be preferred. He not only knows what is best but he also is the final judge.

We will now present God's ways of judging and punishing and your ways of judging and punishing so that you can adjust your ways to God's ways.

God As Judge

As an intelligent mother arranges her home in an orderly way, God has arranged his universe in an orderly way.

God wants his order kept.

If you know for sure what God wants and you deliberately do not do it, you are guilty. If you do not know for sure, you are innocent.

God's way is that simple. If you do not have certain evidence that you have done wrong, the benefit of the doubt is in your favor. God would rather have you plead innocent than guilty.

So the fear or the possibility or a "maybe" or "what if " you have done wrong is not enough. You need more — much more — before accusing yourself of being guilty.

God As Punisher

But if you have such proof that you have sinned, then you are deserving of punishment. Your act of stealing a sizable amount of money or of committing adultery has broken the order God has carefully arranged for everyone's good. Your action has put you out of order and has two kinds of punishment attached to it.

First, being out of order brings its own pain, confusion and worry. Things are not right inside yourself and you know it. Parts of you, instead of you, are running the show. You do not know what wild demands these parts will make. You are like a person on a runaway horse. You have lost control. This is a pain or punishment in itself.

The second kind of punishment is a "reserved" one. Having deliberately chosen to go against God's order, you have set your will against God. God has reserved a punishment for such disobedience. If in your lifetime you do not take back your act of disobedience, then you can rightly fear some form of punishment.

How can you take back your disobedience?

Surprisingly, it is not that difficult.

Since the wrong you did was turning your will away from God, you can make it right by turning back to God. You can do this by telling him you are sorry. "I am sorry, God, because despite how it might look, I love you."

Immediately, and without going to Confession, your disobedience is cancelled. Going to Confession straightens it out officially and gives you a further reassurance that your debt has been forgiven.

Should you refuse to be sorry, the threat of punishment remains until you are.

With God forgiveness is that simple.

You As Judge

As God has an order or arrangement for judging guilt and punishment, so do you.

Unfortunately, because of your panic, your measuring stick is to be perfect. Nothing else will quiet your worrying side.

The accusation, "You could have done it better," repeats itself constantly inside of your head. "It is not good enough. You have to undo it or take it to someone in authority to excuse it."

36

How do you "undo" an action?

You undo an action by erasing it. Like a film that is run backward, you try to retrace the steps of your action by walking or acting backward. Thus, if you walked into a room and a sexual thought occurred to you as you looked at a holy picture, you retrace your steps back to the door and begin again. Somehow you feel this cancels out the whole action, including the sexual thought. It is your way of showing that you wanted no part of it.

Another way of undoing is to repeat an action over and over again until it comes out perfectly.

So, as a judge you cannot allow any inferior actions to pass. You are worried sick until they have been cleansed of the least shadow of guilt. If you cannot handle them yourself and make them perfect, then you feel forced to take them to someone in authority who can handle them and reassure you not to worry about them.

You As Punisher

As a punisher, your worrying side makes you a tyrant.

What kind of punishment does your worrying side inflict on you?

First, you experience a fear that is more than a human being can bear.

Second, you torture yourself by reviewing the same actions over and over again. The questions never stop. "What if this . . .? What if that . . . ? Are you sure . . . ?" After a while your head becomes numb and dumb from worry. When that happens there is nothing to hinder your fear. It takes over completely.

Third, you expose yourself to the worst humiliations possible. In your efforts to be safe, you are often forced to make a fool out of yourself.

Fourth, not having answered or released your fear, you are constantly depressed. The anger that is born from your fear has no place to go. It is pressed down within you; so you feel pressed down or depressed.

These and other forms of torture known only to you are just some of the punishment you experience. Is it any wonder that you always feel on the edge of despair?

Who Will Win?

Obviously, God's ways of judging and punishing are different from yours.

God judges and punishes out of love and for your good. You have nothing to gain by disregarding his wise order and orders.

You judge and punish out of fear and to be safe. You really have nothing to gain by letting panic — instead of common sense — direct you.

God's ways leave you relaxed enough to face life with a whole heart. Of course, at times, you might take advantage of God's goodness and hurt yourself in doing so, but that can be corrected and you can learn from the experience.

Your ways only allow you to face life with half a heart or no heart. Of course, you will be protecting yourself against offending God, but you are destroying yourself in doing so.

So, the crucial question is — whose ways will

win?

You would like to say that God's ways will win, but you are not sure. Actually, you hardly know God. The little that you know about God is based on your own fears or the fearful picture of God presented by your parents and preachers. The picture that you formed in your head is that God is a pretty terrible person when he is angry. So you better not take any chances with him getting angry at you, especially if you feel you have already overexhausted his patience.

How are you going to change your impression of God and be convinced that he will accept your, "I am sorry"?

This is a hard one.

First, you are going to have to deal with the suspicions of your worrying side. "It is too easy a way out."

Second, how can you be sure you really are sorry? A part of you — your easygoing side — does not feel sorry and will probably talk you into doing the same thing again.

Third, you have said it so many times in the past with so little meaning or determination behind it that it was like writing checks with no money in the bank. It is hard for you and others to believe that this act of sorrow is genuine.

So, how can you be sure you are sorry?

The realistic answer is that you can only *try* to be sorry. Start with that. In the beginning, your words might only seem like words to buy off God and your worrying side. But, at least it is a shaky start that can be strengthened as your eyes open to see life as it really is and should be.

Gradually you will see sin as a big swindle that promises much but delivers so little. Seeing that, you will want to change.

So, there is a big difference between God's ways of judging and punishing and yours. God takes into account the fact that you are human and regardless what you have done or been you cannot and should not try to be anything but human.

Chapter Five will spotlight some of the human, God-approved ways of acting that you should follow.

CHAPTER 5
The Human Way

As we have pointed out, despite the insistence of your worrying side, you cannot live life trying to be so careful, so perfect. It will not work because it is not human. You will either become nervous as a leaf in a windstorm or you will stop trying at all. In neither case will you have stopped your panic.

What, then, is the human way to live life?

It will help you to understand what it means to be human if you first clear away some misunderstandings.

Thus, being human is not meant to be an excuse used by your easygoing side to try "to get away with murder." Nor is it meant to justify a careless, irresponsible way of acting. "What did you expect? After all, I am only human."

Nor is it a "shame-on-you" way to make you more serious-minded and worried about your actions. "You should know better. After all, you are not just an animal. You are a human being."

Being human is being accountable only for what you know and are able to accomplish. In this chapter we will direct our attention to these two areas of your life of "knowing" and "doing." In this way, we hope to weaken the fanatical hold your worrying side has on you. If you do not have an exact knowledge of what is expected of you, you can worry yourself into believing that you are expected to accomplish even the impossible.

Knowing Frees

As a human being, your life is greatly

influenced by what you know. If you know the truth about yourself and your relationship with God and others, it is not that difficult to do what is right. Somehow, coming to terms with what is reasonably expected of you, you can find the energies to do it.

So, the important thing is to reasonably come to terms with the truth of what is expected of you.

How do you arrive at the truth?

There are two ways of learning. You can learn from others or you can learn for yourself. To learn from others is quicker, but to learn for yourself is more satisfying. Actually, you should be willing to learn both ways. One places a check on the other.

But, for a number of reasons, you find it a problem to learn either way.

Learning for Yourself

When it comes to truths dealing with religion and sin, you find learning for yourself almost impossible.

The first reason for your difficulty is that you are dealing with an area of life where you have so little personal experience. You have never seen or touched God or sin, so how can you really understand either of them? How can you judge what you have not known personally?

Another reason for your difficulty is that you are dealing with things that are so important that you feel you cannot afford to make a mistake. A part of you might know that a thing is true, but you do not dare judge it for yourself. You cannot take any chances without setting off your panic and upsetment.

So, for both of these reasons, you find yourself depending on others to make your decisions in the area of religion and sin. You feel — and perhaps have been made to feel — that you are too inadequate and too much like a child to trust yourself to come up with the right decision.

Learning from Others

There are several difficulties in having relied only on others to teach you about religion and sin.

First, there is a difficulty with those who taught you. If they were more concerned with impressing you with fear than with facts, then they were overdeveloping the worrying side of you. Their total concern was that you keep God's law. Obviously, this concentration on fear and the law would not leave you much room to develop as a person.

Second, in relying only on others, you are stuck with whatever they taught you, regardless when you learned it. Thus, that which you learned as a child and with a child's limitations might still be influencing your actions as an adult. You can still remember what Sister said and how important she made it sound that you do exactly as she said. Even now, you feel a fright inside of you if you do not do an action exactly as you learned it. Somehow in this area of religion and sin you do not feel free to bring what you learned up to date.

Third, relying on others to make your decisions about sin, you must keep in constant contact with them and burden them and yourself with the thousand and one details you feel they should know to make an accurate judgment about your action or doubt.

For these and other reasons, it is not wise or really human to rely so totally on others to make your decisions about religion and sin.

The Final Decision

Regardless when and who taught you about religion and sin, this is your religious training and it is important for you. Those teachings should give you the kind of protection that fence posts give to a highway. They help to keep you on the road.

So, you have a need for these teachings from others. But you should use these teachings as a "starting point," and not the "finish line" of your own thinking. It is what *you* finally decide that should count. It is this decision coming from you that makes you "human" and not just a trained animal.

"But, I am too scared to make such important decisions or judgments on my own. How can I be sure whether what I have done is right or wrong?"

Your fears about deciding what is right and wrong are understandable. Several chapters from now we will discuss the areas of sex, harming others, stealing, thoughts and feelings, and some religious practices to help you make your decisions about what is right and what is wrong.

But for now, it is important that you impress on yourself that the privilege and duty of making the final decisions on sin is yours.

If you know that what you have done is wrong, then that is your decision. No "ifs," "ands," or "buts" about it, it is wrong.

But, if when you are trying to decide whether something is wrong, you come up with the answers, "I do not know" or "I have a doubt" or "I am not sure," then — despite your panic to play it safe and plead guilty — you should not accuse yourself of being wrong. Before God, as in civil courts, you are innocent until proven guilty.

Therefore

Thus, if you are doubting whether you committed a sin, harmed anyone, confessed correctly, or have some obligation, the benefit of the doubt is in your favor. You should convince yourself that you did not commit the sin, harm anyone, did confess correctly, and do not have the obligation.

Should you be wrong, it does not matter. God will not hold you accountable.

"But," you might object, "I will not be able to convince my worrying side to stop worrying."

Maybe you won't be able to convince your worrying side in the beginning, but gradually this side of you will let up. Gradually the truth will free you and you will be able to take back control over yourself.

"But," you might object again, "will this not give too much freedom to the easygoing side of me?"

46

It might seem that way, but that is not so. You are not so unconcerned about sin as you might feel you are. After all, regardless of your motives, if you really did not care about committing sin, you would not be scrupulous. As a matter of fact, letting up on your worrying side will take away some of the need of your easygoing side to break loose. It has run wild because it was so tied down by your worrying side.

So, you have some attitudes to change if you want to be human. You must learn to judge for yourself and give yourself the benefit of the doubt and declare yourself "not guilty" on the basis of these doubts.

When It Comes to Doing

When it comes to the area of "doing," it is one thing to know what is right and another to do it.

For example, it is one thing to know that an uncontrolled sex life or drinking problem must be brought under control; it is another to do it, and to do it humanly. There will be needed a fuller realization of the harm that is being caused, some time to develop a certain amount of discipline, and probably a number of failures before such control can be obtained.

So, the sayings of parents and preachers, "If you know what is right, you should be able to do it" or "if you really put your mind to it, you can do it," are not always true. Maybe you can do it eventually, but not necessarily now.

Realizing that "doing" does not follow automatically from "knowing," you can slow down some of the rush of your worrying side to make things right — and even perfect — immediately.

There is time to work out what needs working out.

In the meantime, a simple, "I will try," is sufficient to satisfy God that you have some intention to change. God does not ask for anything more. Why, then, should you?

The fact of the matter is that to try to do more, so quickly, would be inhuman. Excessive, consuming fear and panic might be able to bring about an immediate change, but it would also bring more complications than are healthy.

So, whether it is a fault that needs correcting or the paying off of large sums of money cheated from an insurance company or whatever, the human way is to proceed slowly but surely, not with an all-consuming panic.

Faults and Feelings

Two important areas of your life that must be accepted as a part of your humanity are your faults and feelings.

Regardless how much your worrying side wants nothing to do with your faults and those feelings that are not "nice," to be human you have to accept the fact that both your faults and feelings are a part of you. They cannot be ignored or denied without hurting you.

Faults

No matter how much you worry or how cautious you are, you are capable of making mistakes. Maybe your excessive worry might keep you away from obvious, external faults, but you are destroying yourself in the process.

So, if you are going to accept your humanity, you have to make room in your life for faults. You have been turning your head into a pressure cooker trying to avoid them. It is a wonder your head has not exploded.

Obviously, this accepting of your faults is not an excuse to go looking for what is wrong or not to make a sincere effort to do what is right. No, it is simply accepting the fact that God only expects you to use "ordinary" care to avoid what is wrong and to do what is right.

Thus, if you have no real reasons to assume you left the gas on, then you should *presume* you did not. That is ordinary care. To go back and check the stove out of fear that you *might* have left it on is not using ordinary care. It is foolishly giving into your worrying side. Should you find out later that you left the gas on, you are at fault but you have not sinned.

Even in areas where you have sinned because you deliberately did not use ordinary care to do what is right, it is not the end of the world. Quietly and quickly as possible start *now* to do what is right. Try not to panic as the voice of your worrying side screams at you with a voice of doom, "If you had listened to me and had been more careful, this would not have happened." Taking a lot of time listening to this side of you is wasting a lot of time.

So, accepting your faults — whether they are sins or not — is a big part of being human.

Feelings

If, as a human being, your life is greatly influenced by what you know, it is even more influenced by how you feel.

So, it is vital for you to understand and accept the part your feelings play in your life. We will first consider the problem your feelings present and then how to treat them.

The Problem

Being so greatly influenced by your feelings, you become extremely uneasy when you begin to have feelings that could lead you to commit serious sin. Your worrying side wants you to have nothing to do with such feelings. Just having such feelings is like lighting a match around gasoline. The situation becomes too dangerous to control.

Because of this fear, you and your teachers looked on certain feelings as if they were sins in themselves. So you do not want them to enter your head. You shake your head or strain yourself not to feel them or, if you have felt them, to get rid of them. If you fail to keep them out or get rid of them immediately, you feel you have sinned. The tension you put yourself through in treating your feelings so severely is a serious problem.

How to Treat Them

The best way to treat your feelings is to understand them and to accept them.

To understand your feelings, you should realize that they are only the reports of your eyes, ears, touch, and appetites telling you about the "pleasing" or "displeasing" qualities of people and things. You feel attracted toward what is pleasing and want nothing to do with what is displeasing.

To accept your feelings, you should realize that their reports are important to you. You should also realize that your feelings are neither right nor wrong. They simply are telling you how things are. They are not sinful.

So, regardless what influence your feelings can have on you, you have a need for your feelings to exist and to make their reports without interference or censorship. It is far better for you to feel your feelings and handle them openly than to try to suppress them and have them gang up and overpower you.

Accepting Mixed Feelings

This acceptance of your feelings means that you should recognize and accept the fact that you can have mixed feelings or mixed reports about people and things, regardless how important or sacred these persons or things might be.

Thus, depending on whether they are giving you pleasure or pain, you can like and hate a parent, a marriage partner, a friend.

You can like and hate yourself and God.

You can like and hate a job, a home, a part of a country.

You can be glad for a person and jealous of her.

You can feel angry at a person and sorry for him.

In a few words, you can have "mixed" feelings about everyone and everything. This is normal. These feelings should be allowed to make their reports. Despite the objections and embarrassment of your worrying side over how bad it looks to have such "bad" feelings, having such feelings is a part of being human. It is not sinful.

Accepting Sexual Feelings

A very important — but often confusing — area of your feelings that you must accept to be truly human is the area of sexual feelings.

As a human being you are a "sexual" person. You are either male or female and if you are normal, you will often have sexual feelings toward others.

It is vital that you accept the reports of your sex feelings. To block out or deny their reports is like blinding your eyes or deafening your ears. That would be totally unreasonable and inhuman. So it is important for you to realize that you will not find a way out of your panic by denying the existence of your sexual feelings. Such a denial of sex only makes matters worse and has you considering a part of you as bad. Obviously, that cannot be healthy.

"But," you ask, "although having feelings, even sex feelings, are not sins, does not sin enter somewhere? Is it not sinful to consent to sexual or other 'bad' feelings?"

How feelings can become sins will be treated in Chapter Seven where sex feelings are considered at length. What is said about sex feelings applies to all feelings. In this chapter, our concern is to show that feelings are not sinful. They are a necessary part of your humanity and must be allowed to exist and make their reports without interference.

You in Control

A final, and perhaps the most important, truth about yourself as a human being is to realize that despite the control your worrying side or your easygoing side can have over you, they are not *you*. They are only two sides of you supplying you with information from two different sides of life. They are like two ears listening to sounds from two different directions.

Your worrying side listens to the echo of the voices of your parents, teachers, and preachers. It tells you what they would want you to do or be. "Do not do that. Do this. You should have known better. You are no good."

Your easygoing side listens to the child in you. It listens to what you like and dislike. "I want that pleasure. I don't want any pain. Why can't I have what I want, now? Just pretend everything is going to be alright, and it will be. Do not worry about anything."

These are the constant reports you get from these two sides of you. They are good reports and you should listen to them. But, they are only reports. They are not you.

You are so much more.

So, the important thing is to realize that "you" exist and that you are more than the voices of these two sides of you.

You are you.

And it is up to you to make your final decisions.

It is also important for you to realize that — regardless how you decide — the side that was not chosen will still be there and will want what it wanted. Thus, should you follow the warnings of your worrying side and look away from a sexually attractive person, your easygoing side will still want you to look and feel sexual pleasures for that person. Such feelings are normal. They are not going to go away just because you decided to follow the warnings of your worrying side. So, no matter how intensely you feel those feelings and how intensely you desire that person, that does not destroy the sincerity of your looking away. It is *you* who are looking away, despite the feelings and desires of your easygoing side.

In Chapter Six, we will consider the existence of "you" more at length. Too many times in your life and choices, you have only been the shadow following the lead of either your worrying side or easygoing side. As much as is possible, it is time for you to take over the control of your life.

CHAPTER 6

Getting Control
over Yourself

Although as a human being you were made in a special way by God, you do not feel special. You do not feel anything. At most, you feel horrible and worthless. You are so eaten alive with fears and doubts that you feel next to dead inside. You cannot laugh. You cannot relax. You cannot do anything but worry.

Something is very wrong.

Something desperately needs correcting.

What is wrong with you?

Perhaps you can begin to understand what is wrong if you listen carefully to the words that are constantly in your mind and on your lips. "I am afraid. I am worried."

What are your words saying?

They are saying, "I have become *fear*. I have become *worry*. I am not John or Mary. No, I am fear. I am worry. I am being completely controlled by my fears and worries. *I* am not in control. My fears and worries are. They are running me."

Finding You

To get control over yourself, it will help to clear away who you are not and then try to establish who you are.

First, as we considered at the end of the last chapter, you are neither your worrying side nor your easygoing side. They are sides of you, not you.

Second, you are not just a group of individual parts that have been allowed to run you. You are more than your fears, your hunger for food, your urges for sex, and so many other parts of you. They are parts of you; they are not you.

58

Third, nor are you what people think of you or want you to be. You are so afraid of others and their opinion of you that most of the time you would rather please them than be yourself. Their opinion of you takes over and controls you.

If you are not one of these three influences, then who are you?

You are you.

You use the word "I" to express how you are different from *sides* of you, *parts* of you, or *others*. *I* am not my worrying or easygoing side. *I* am not my hunger, sex urges, or fears. *I* am not anyone else.

It is your "I" that you must be made more aware of and that must take over control of you. Sides of you or parts of you or others cannot be allowed to control you and act as you. You should listen to all of them and consider the valuable information they bring you, but the final deciding of what you are going to do must depend on your "I." "I am going to run me, not my sides, parts, or others."

Developing "I" Control

Actually, this realizing that your "I" should be in control of you is not totally new to you. Look at how many times you have said, "I am speaking. I am walking. I am worrying." Are not your words saying that your "I" should be directing and controlling your speaking, walking, and worrying? Obviously, it is not your speaking, walking, or worrying that should be controlling your "I."

So your "I" is a power that is capable of controlling your many parts and actions.

"But, what if my 'I' is not controlling me? What if my worries, impulses, or what others think of me are controlling me? How can I get control over me?"

It is a gradual process.

First, you start by realizing that you have such a power.

Second, you begin to exercise this power of "I" control in small things. Supposing you have a problem of eating too much or of eating the wrong kinds of food. You should ask yourself the question, "Who is going to win? Am *I* going to win or is my appetite for food going to win?" If you let your appetite for food — a part of you — win, you lose. If your "I" wins, that is a real victory. You have increased your "I" control.

Third, having learned some "I" control in small actions, you can begin to apply this control to your fears over sin. Something may need to be done about your past sinful life, but who is going to direct what needs to be done — your fear or your "I"? Hopefully, you will arrive at a point where you can say, "I am in control, not my fear. I'll do what needs doing, not my panic."

Your "I" Makes You Different

It is your "I" that makes you different from others. "I am doing this, not you. I am different from you."

Although this truth that you are different from everyone else is so simple and obvious, it can play a big part in getting over your scrupulous condition.

A great part of your problem is that you are still depending on others to do for you what you should be doing for yourself. You are especially depending on them to make judgments for you and to take away your fears. Because you are hurting so badly, you want the "big people" in your life to take over and make everything right and safe again.

Of course, to ask for help from others from time to time is very understandable and very human. At times of confusion or crisis, it is even necessary. But you are not going to solve your problems or grow by always relying on someone else to reassure you that everything is alright. That would be giving someone else the control over your life that should be coming from you, from your "I." You might as well become that other person. Obviously, that is not going to really solve anything.

For this reason, "blind obedience" to your confessor is not going to solve anything.

First of all, it probably will not work because something inside of you will resist it or not be able to follow it perfectly.

Secondly, if you could become so obedient, what have you really accomplished as far as improving your condition? Not that much. In fact, it would hold you back from growing and getting "I" control. Such obedience would keep you as dependent as a child and make you a shadow of someone else. Its crippling complications of overdependency are too numerous to mention here.

So letting another take over control and make your decisions about sin is alright as a temporary measure. It can give you some relief from your excessive fear. It even takes on a value as a virtue and is approved of by God. But it is not a very good permanent solution. It is better than nothing, but, hopefully, a better way can be found.

That better way is through "I" control.

So, the first step toward getting control over yourself is to realize that you have this power of "I" control. Each time you use it, the stronger you get.

The Help Anger Gives

A second step to getting control is to realize that one of the main sources of your "I" power is your ability to get angry and to use your anger to help you. This needs explaining.

Of all the forces inside of you, you find your fears the most difficult to handle. Your fears make you so tense inside that they can make you feel sick to your stomach.

This is unfortunate. Fear was intended by nature to help you, not to hurt you.

Fear is a dynamo of energy that gives you the power to do one of two things. It helps you to run away from danger or it helps you to get angry enough to fight the danger. In either case, your nerves and muscles get alerted to act. If you do not run away or fight off the danger, your nerves stay alerted and tense for hours and even days.

And when your nerves do relax, if the danger is still there or reoccurs, you become alerted and tense as soon as you become aware of it. So doing nothing about a danger usually solves nothing. It only keeps you on edge.

Most use their fear power to run away. But surprisingly, they run from their fears and not from the danger. Thus, they pretend that there really is nothing to be afraid of or they distract themselves from considering what they are afraid of.

This wanting to run away is what hits you first when you are afraid. You want to run away from sin or anything that looks like sin. But where can you run? You can see sin in almost everything and everyone, so where can you go to be safe? To a monastery? Not only is it doubtful that you could live such a life, but, even if you could, would you be safe there? Probably not.

So, running away is not always a good answer to your problems.

The Better Answer

A better answer would be that when fear strikes to put on the brakes of anger. "I am not going to run away. I am going to face what needs facing. I am sick and tired of always running away. I am angry enough to do something about things."

This anger determination will not come all at once. You will find yourself automatically slipping into the easier habit of running away rather than stand and fight. But the power is there to be used. A confessor would probably help you more by insisting that you get angry at yourself and fight what you are afraid of than to get angry at you for not following the obedience he has imposed.

What is it that is frightening you? Is it sins you have committed or might commit? Then get angry; and, with your confessor's help, come to terms with what has to be done. Then do it. Stop running away from it.

The Next Step

After working up your anger to face what needs facing, your next step is to see exactly what is expected of you in the different areas of your life. Confused or unsure knowledge is not good enough. It only makes your fears worse. But exact knowledge lets you know where you stand. You might not like what you see, but it is better for you to know than to overdo just to be sure. Once you know, you can apply your "I" power and anger to doing it.

To give you exact, detailed knowledge of some of the more difficult areas of your life, we will give a whole chapter to a consideration of sex, fear of harming others, stealing, Confession, and purpose of amendment. Each of these chapters will consider the examples of Bruce, Jean, Timothy, Ann, and Michael of Chapter Two.

(Perhaps it would be good to reread the case history of each of the above before beginning the chapter which concerns them.)

CHAPTER 7

The Christian and Sex

We chose Bruce and his problems with sex as our first consideration because sex is the downfall of most scrupulous people.

It is not surprising that sex should present problems.

As an intense pleasure, it is hard to find any other pleasure that is more intense.

As a responsibility, sex must be treated seriously. Sex is the only source of life. It must be guarded if the continuance of the human race is to be insured.

As an expression of love, sex must be meaningful or lose its real purpose for being.

So sex is more than a toy. A toy can be used or abused, without serious consequences. Sex cannot.

And yet, there must be a balance.

At times sex can even have a light or humorous side to it.

More important, sex is a part of us and must be accepted as such. So sex should never be ignored, even though it is not being used. It is like a house that is not being used presently. Nevertheless, it must be given proper attention. To totally disregard the house is to render it unfit for later use. So, too, with sex. It cannot be ignored without serious consequences.

A Statement of Truth

To really *will* to commit an act of sex alone or with someone who is not your partner in marriage is a serious offense against yourself and society. It is a lack of control over yourself or a lack of caring of what happens to others or society and the sacredness of marriage.

To clear our view of this truth, we must separate what really are sexual sins from those actions that might look like sexual sins but are not.

Clearing the View

First, there are many things that deal with sex that are not sins.

A knowledge of sex and sexual activity is not a sin. It is something that everyone should know.

"But," you reply, "when I read or talk about sex, I am stimulated sexually. I feel that is wrong."

No, it is not wrong. The pleasure you feel is both natural and normal. It is God who attached this pleasure to sex knowledge, so it cannot be wrong.

"But, you do not understand. I like and want the pleasure I feel. I enjoy it. In fact, I am only reading or talking about sex to get aroused. Surely that is wrong."

Yes, if that is the *only* reason for your reading or talking about sex, then you have done something wrong. Although you have not performed an external act of sex, you have sinned. Since you are only doing what you are doing to arouse yourself, then you are *willing* something wrong.

But, if your reading, thinking, or talking about sex is for any other purpose than to arouse yourself sexually, then you have not sinned.

So, if you are reading or thinking about sex to learn more about sex or to enjoy its humor in a joke, you have not sinned.

Or, if you allow yourself to feel sex to air out your feelings so as not to be so tense about sex, you have not sinned.

Or, if sex feelings accompany a demonstration of affection and love, you have not sinned.

What Makes the Difference?

So wishing, wanting, liking, and enjoying sex feelings are not sins, as long as they are not the main purpose of your action.

There would be something wrong if you did not wish, want, like, or enjoy sexual feelings. These are natural, normal feelings and they have a right to exist and be felt. To suppress or ignore them is only asking for trouble. If they are not allowed to come through directly, they will find other ways of being felt. It is better to deal with them out in the open than to have them catch you off guard by attaching themselves to other things such as holy pictures, etc.

"But, even if it is not wrong to feel the sex feelings that accompany learning, laughing, airing out sex feelings, or demonstrating affection, is it not wrong to expose myself to the danger of being overcome by sex? Is not that a proximate danger and a sin in itself? Is not that what the preachers warned about?"

Although allowing your sex feelings to come through could be a danger for you, it is better to let them come through. By trying to keep them out of your head and thoughts, you are creating worse dangers for yourself. You have become so obsessed in trying to stay clear of any sex feelings or thoughts that you can hardly think of anything else.

So, no matter how intensely such feelings are felt or how long they stay, they are not sins. Feelings and thoughts are not sins. If your reading, thinking, talking, and actions are being done for a good reason, then continue to do them.

Applying This to Bruce

Because of Bruce's upset state of mind, it might not be wise or even possible to insist on these truths about sex.

First of all, Bruce has become so frightened of sex that he panics at anything that slightly resembles sex. Even words that are innocent in themselves but could have a double or sexual meaning terrify him. As if sex had become a contagious, deadly disease, he wants no part of it.

Obviously, then, to point out that the wishing, wanting, liking, and enjoying of the sex feelings that accompany his actions are not sins is not going to help. He is too terrified to have anything to do with sex.

Actually, Bruce feels a need to terrify himself over sex. He feels that this is the only way he can be pure. He does not trust himself enough to come near sex. So, even if Bruce could accept the truth that feelings and thoughts about sex are not sins, it would not help. He is being stubborn about wanting nothing to do with sex because he is scared. Bruce knows his weakness and it is that fear that is making him stubborn.

Where to Begin?

Where can Bruce begin in handling his sex problem?

He has tried to run away from sex, but that is not helping. Our society is too filled with sex to successfully avoid all sex reminders. Besides, it is not normal or healthy to totally cut off an awareness of something as natural as sex.

So running away is not a good answer.

Nor is trying to slow Bruce down enough to discuss and face sex a good answer. He is not strong enough to handle so much fear.

What can be done for Bruce?

Helps

First, Bruce must be reassured that his efforts to do what is right are pleasing to God, even though he is giving in to his fears.

Second, it should be pointed out that his fears are partly correct. Obviously, as he himself realizes, his life has not been a good one. Thanks to his fears, he is now trying to change it.

So, some fear has a place in his life.

But his fear is much too loud. Like a clock, fear has set off an alarm to awaken him. Now the fear must be toned down. He cannot live in a constant state of alarm.

Third, for Bruce to put his fear back into its rightful place will require some repairs on his personality. Which is stronger — he as a person or his fears? Surprisingly, just the asking of this question is a help. Obviously, he as a person should be stronger. If he can work up enough anger and determination that no part of him is going to rule him, he — not his fear — will eventually win. He should be encouraged to look at newspapers, magazines, and television with this determination that he, and not his fear, is going to win. So he gets sexual feelings and desires. Once again, he — not his feelings or desires — is going to win.

In the Meantime

Until some of this awareness that he is a person comes through, all efforts should be made to slow down Bruce's panic. To do this, Bruce's confessor might have to declare him as not responsible for his present supposed or actual sins of sex.

This statement about his not being responsible should be made in writing.

Next, the roots of Bruce's panic must be exposed. Why is Bruce so terrified over sin? Is it because he really understands the harm sin causes to others and to himself? Probably not.

The first and surface reason why Bruce is terrified of hell is the threat of the horrible physical pain that would await him.

The next and perhaps stronger reason for Bruce's panic over sin is that he was taught that to go to hell is to be rejected and be lonely forever.

To be so rejected is more than Bruce could bear. As a matter of fact, so much of the reason why Bruce reached out sexually to anyone was to prove that he was acceptable. Bruce had to constantly prove this to others and to himself because not to be acceptable was to be lonely and scared. He could not stand that.

So Bruce reached out sexually to others because that was the only meaningful way that Bruce had for reaching out. It made him feel important and in control of the other. Somehow, even though he paid for sex or reached out to someone inferior, his having control over someone made him feel secure enough not to feel alone and helpless. After all, he was in charge and that gave him a sense of power.

His being still craves for that sense of power and being important and not to be alone. That is why his sexual thoughts and desires are so strong. They are more than thoughts or desires about sex. They are more a plea for others to care and accept him.

So, the important question is, can Bruce's loneliness be filled by relating to actual people now? If it could, then Bruce would not be so strongly drawn to live in the past and daydream about his many sexual adventures.

So, it is not just a misunderstanding about the sinfulness of his sexual thoughts and desires that needs correcting. Something should be done to correct Bruce's lonely condition. Having people around him would probably prove more helpful than a lot of preaching about how he has to snap out of it and stop withdrawing into himself.

So

If dealing with your sexual thoughts and feelings has you in a state of panic, try to realize that your sexual thoughts and feelings are not sins. If you are having those thoughts or feelings for any other reason than just to arouse yourself sexually, then do not worry about them.

If you find yourself avoiding newspapers, magazines, or television because something sexual might appear, then ask yourself who is going to win. Are your fears going to win or are you going to win? Do not give up until you win.

If you find yourself in Bruce's position of withdrawing from everyone because of a fear of sex, force yourself to get out to people. Withdrawing is not decreasing your panic; it is only increasing it.

Your coping with your fears about sex is a difficult task. Realize that God knows this and will not be forgetful of your efforts to arrive at a sensible solution.

CHAPTER 8

The Christian and Anger

Another serious trap for scrupulous people is the fear of harming others. Our example of Jean is quite common (see Chapter Two).

Jean's feelings of harming others can have several explanations.

Her fears of harming others could arise from the fact that she has harmed someone in the past but paid little or no attention to it. In fact, she forgot all about it. Now it is showing itself in a fear of harming others.

Or, Jean's fears could result from having been blamed so much in her life she is afraid that if anything happens — even though it is an accident — she will be blamed for it. She cannot take any chances of anything happening, even if it is an accident. So she checks and rechecks the gas and anything that could be dangerous.

Or, Jean's fears could be the result of her mistaken idea of how much power she has. Her imagination is running wild.

Thus she is afraid that if she says the word "evil" or "devil" that she causes whatever she happens to be looking at to become evil or given over to the devil. Or if something bad pops into her head and she then thinks of someone, she is afraid that something bad will happen to that person.

It sounds kind of childish, but it can seem real to Jean. She is terrified that it might be true.

Or, along this childish way of thinking, Jean's fears of harming others could really be her fears that others are out to harm her or not be that careful about her safety. So her precautions are really the precautions she would want others to take about her. In other words, she is trying to protect others in the same way she would want to be protected. She would want them to check and recheck to make sure her world is safe.

Most Likely

But the most likely explanation is that her fears of *actually* harming others are simply trying to express the unexpressed resentments she has toward others. She really does not *will* to harm them. She only wants to tell them how she feels they have hurt her. But because she does not want to displease them and turn them away from her, she cannot speak out her desire to want to hurt them as they have hurt her. This needs some explaining.

Because of her training, Jean will not only not express anger; she will not even allow herself to *feel* angry. What would be normal anger feelings in someone else comes out as nervousness or down-feelings in Jean.

So, Jean's anger is kept hidden, even from herself.

But let a situation that contains the slightest possibility of harming someone arise and Jean becomes all upset. She has to check and recheck her actions to be totally sure she is not harming anyone or wishing evil on him.

Why is Jean's fear of harming someone so great? Why is Jean so afraid of not turning off the gas properly?

That Suspenseful Moment

Actually, it is not the gas or other possible dangers that are so upsetting to Jean. Rather, it is her hidden anger. This anger is just waiting to strike out at someone, especially at someone who is a cause of conflict, concern, or annoyance. Because Jean cannot allow even occasional blow-ups or disagreements in her dealings with others, she carries this trapped anger and its desires to harm others inside of her. Leaving the gas on would be an opportunity for getting back at others.

Of course, Jean does not choose to leave the gas on, but for a suspenseful moment inside herself her anger had a possible outlet. And even though she was not consciously aware of what was happening, she was aware that something was not right. This something — her hidden anger — is what is giving her the fear that she actually might have harmed or desired to harm someone or give him over to evil.

But, because she cannot allow herself to feel her anger and say to herself, "Yes, I would like to hurt you as I feel you have hurt me," the anger and the fear that she has harmed someone remains.

Jean does not know what to do. She tries desperately to convince herself and others that she would never want to harm anyone. But, somehow, Jean is not satisfied with her own arguments. So, she feels a need to run to someone to convince her that it is impossible for her to have harmed anyone. This reassurance helps for a while, but Jean is never really satisfied because she has not seen that her hidden anger is behind her feelings of guilt.

Only when Jean realizes that her desires to harm others who have hurt her are normal will her guilt and panic go away.

Fear and Anger

To see how normal Jean's anger and desires of harming others are, recall what we said in Chapter Six about fear and anger.

A person cannot become angry unless she is afraid.

Her fear could be over the loss of some convenience, a good name, competence, money, health, having her own way, etc.

As we said, when a person is threatened with such a loss, her first impulse is to pretend that everything is O.K.

If that does not work, then she might try to run away from whatever is threatening her.

If running away is not possible, her final weapon against fear is anger. Her body prepares for a fight in an attempt to destroy the threat.

This anger and desire of wanting to harm what is threatening her is a normal reaction that should be spontaneous. Although as a human being and as a Christian the person needs to control the harm her anger would want to cause, her anger should be allowed to exist and have its say inside her head.

Neither Right nor Wrong

Applying this to Jean and to yourself, it is important for you to realize that since your anger feelings arise spontaneously to help you overcome fear, such feelings are neither right nor wrong. They just are. And they have a right to be — regardless whether they are directed at God, parents, family, or friends.

You are wrong or guilty when you allow your anger feelings to control you or force you to act unjustly.

But as long as your anger feelings are under control, they are not wrong. In fact, they are a natural resource. Used constructively to slow you down and give you backbone when fear strikes, your anger feelings give you the power you need to face the more scary parts of life.

A Way of Acting

As you might suspect, Jean's problem is deeper than an incorrect knowledge of anger.

Jean is confused about herself as a lady.

A lady is not all sweetness and kindness. Before all else, a lady is a human being. She is not immune from fear and anger.

Jean is also confused about herself as a Christian.

A Christian is not without feelings. A Christian might turn the other cheek, but she can still *feel* like knocking the block off the person who slapped her with his hand or critical remarks.

So, if Jean wants to get rid of her fear of harming people or wishing them over to evil, she has to come down from her ideal world.

If Jean can accept her natural feelings of wanting to strike out at those who are upsetting her, she will not have to conceal her feelings and be afraid they will pop up in actions that have some danger attached.

Too Much of the Child

But Jean will have to do more than come down from her ideal world. She will also have to come up out of her childish world.

Jean's runaway imagination is like that of a child.

In her imagination Jean believes that she has powers that she really does not have. She cannot make anyone "evil." Nor can she harm anyone by her thoughts or wishes. She simply does not have that kind of power.

It would be good for Jean to remind herself that her powers to harm others are tremendously exaggerated. In fact, they are not even real. They are the product of her runaway imagination. They are the child part of her that is supposing or "making believe." They should not be taken seriously.

Patience

Obviously, Jean — and you if this fear of harming others is a problem for you — is not going to be able to correct her situation all at once. She has become such an expert in cutting off her anger feelings that she does it automatically. It will take effort and patience for her to allow such feelings to come through. It will also take effort and patience before she can learn to bring her runaway, childish imagination under control.

So efforts and patience are needed on the part of both Jean and her counselor.

To counsel Jean to be patient with her

problem until her anger feelings can come through normally might sound strange. In many ways Jean is in her present difficulty because she has exercised too much patience. She has been so patient and understanding that there has not been any room for anger.

It would seem that Jean could use some impatience. Actually she can, and her impatience should be directed at her overcautious rechecking of danger. She should scold herself and say, "What am I doing rechecking the gas? I am acting like an idiot or a three-year-old who cannot be trusted to know better. Of course the gas is off."

Acting Against

So, along with an understanding and correcting of her wrong ideas about anger, Jean must begin to apply some brakes to her fears.

Jean's fears are not going to stop themselves.

Nor is it likely that God will work a miracle to stop them. God is not going to do what Jean can do for herself.

Stopping her fears is up to Jean. She must gradually slow down to see the difference between "feeling" and "thinking." She *feels* she might be harming someone, but she really does not *know* or *think* so. Nevertheless, to satisfy her fears or feelings, she rechecks the gas.

No matter how necessary this rechecking seems, it has to stop.

Despite the pleading of her fears, Jean cannot afford to give in to them. At most, in the beginning, she could be allowed to check the gas once. No more. This must be insisted on. It will be hard and even seem cruel, but it must be done. Both Jean and the counselor must be firm in their determination to stop this unreasonable panic-giving-into-fear.

Being Honest

Next, Jean must be encouraged to talk about her resentments.

"Do you resent what your mother did? Do you feel at times that you hate her? Are there times you feel that you want to hurt her?"

Jean's first response to these questions will probably be, "No." She would consider herself bad, disloyal, or unloving if she said, "Yes."

Would Jean be bad, disloyal, or unloving if she had such unpleasant feelings toward her mother? No. She would only be allowing some of her humanity to come through. Everyone is capable of such feelings. They are the negative side of her mixed feelings toward another.

So, Jean should be encouraged to speak freely about her feelings. It is better to have such feelings out in the open than to hide them and have them hook onto the first action that has some danger attached to it.

If Jean can admit and accept such feelings as normal, she will have come a long way toward maturing. The world we live in — whether outside or inside ourselves — is not always a pleasant one. To accept the world and to accept herself as not always being pleasant is a part of her growing up. It is leaving the dreamy, safe world of childhood behind.

CHAPTER 9

The Christian and Stealing

Another quicksand area of panic for the scrupulous person is the area of stealing. Our example of Timothy in Chapter Two is rather common.

If there was one thing that Timothy was taught as a child, it was that stealing is both bad and painful. Having stolen a dollar from his mother's pocketbook to treat himself to ice cream and a soda, Timothy was caught and spanked by his father. He had been told that he was being punished more for the principle than for the money. It was hoped that he would learn a lesson.

A Simple Truth

That stealing or taking what belongs to someone else is wrong is obvious. It is a violation of the rights of others. What has been taken should be returned.

How seriously wrong is stealing?

It depends on the amount of harm that is caused to another person. The norms determining the amount of harm caused to another depend upon situations and circumstances. Your counselor or confessor is well acquainted with these commonly accepted rules.

This rule for stealing is rather simple and easy to apply when it involves taking money from an individual. It is not so simple or easy to apply when you are dealing with something other than money or when you are dealing with a group.

We will give a special consideration to some cases dealing with something other than money or with a group.

Working for Another

In working for another there is not an exchange of money for money, rather the exchange is money for labor.

The employer and the worker determine the wage to be given for a number of days of work. That they can do easy enough. What is not so easy to determine is how hard the employee will work. Too many factors of health, abilities, and attitudes can affect how hard the person will be able to work. So, if the employer or his foreman knows that an employee is sleeping on the job, leaving early, not working as hard as he could, and even taking things home, he can allow this. After all, it is his company.

Since the employer could check up, correct, and even fire a worker for such conduct but does not, then the worker is not cheating or stealing. He has the employer's permission to do what he is doing.

So, although Timothy should have done a good day's work for a good day's pay out of a respect for his own dignity as a responsible person, as a matter of fact, he is not guilty of stealing and he does not have to repay his employer.

Health Plans

In regard to the arrangement of doctors to put a fee on a health insurance form that is higher than they would actually charge a patient who is not covered by a health plan, this practice is neither cheating nor stealing.

Since in a doctor-patient relationship you are

dealing with an exchange of highly technical services for money, it is difficult to set an exact price on such services. What would determine the price? Would you base it on the time actually spent with the patient or the years of studies and preparation that were needed to give the patient professional service?

It is difficult to determine a fair exchange of money for such services. Common practice, the ability of the patient to pay, and the doctor's own sense of dedication all enter in determining the fee.

Now, if a doctor charges a patient a maximum fee because he is in a health plan, he is within his rights. Those supervising the plan can review the case and make some kind of adjustment if they believe the fee is too high.

So, Timothy is not cheating or stealing when he takes advantage of the doctor's willingness to settle for the fee granted through the health plan.

Insurances

Along similar lines, the rules of stealing are somewhat different when dealing with insurance companies than when dealing with money taken from an individual.

Insurance companies are in business to make a profit. They establish the conditions that they feel will make them the best profit.

Now, suppose a person wants to have his car insured but he has already had several accidents. To insure it under his own name would result in paying an extremely high price for the insurance. He might feel that this is unjust because those accidents occurred under conditions that really were not his fault. Still those accidents are credited to him and he needs insurance to be able to drive.

What is he to do?

Suppose he talks it over with his sister and she agrees to register his car and insurance under her name. Is that cheating? What if he has an accident that costs the insurance company a considerable amount of money? Can he with an honest conscience allow them to pay the costs? Suppose he lies about some of the details of the accident. Would he still be allowed to let them pay?

These and other questions can arise from such a situation.

The answer to all of these questions is, "No, he is not stealing and does not have to repay damages done to an insurance company." He might be guilty of lying, but that is not stealing.

The reason why he is not stealing is that legally speaking the car belongs to his sister. She can keep and do with the car whatever she pleases. She can let him take it or not. It is up to the insurance company to prove that the car is not hers. If they cannot or do not want to waste the time or money investigating the matter more deeply, that is their right.

So, if this case applies to Timothy, he is not stealing.

Paying Taxes

Likewise, Timothy would not be guilty of stealing if he did not pay the full amount of taxes the government would claim of him.

This needs explaining.

The duties of patriotism require that each of us shoulder our fair share of government expenses. As Christ indicated, "Give to Caesar the things that belong to Caesar."

What is a fair share for an individual?

It would seem that a fair share should take into account the benefits the individual has received and his ability to shoulder a full responsibility. His earnings are an indication of both.

So, in general, he should pay what he is taxed.

However, if for a valid reason he *cannot* pay the full amount or does not believe he has an obligation to support the government in its expenses to wage an unjust war, provide abortion services and the like, he is not obligated to pay the full amount. He might not be considered patriotic, but he would not be stealing.

Unemployment Compensation

Similarly, Timothy is not stealing if he works a side job while collecting unemployment compensation.

Actually, it is better for him to be working than not to be working. To lie around and possibly lose his desire to work is not healthy.

But, more to the point, the unemployment compensation is an emergency measure to help him over a difficult time. He has nothing to say about its conditions. He cannot claim more should the amount given be insufficient to maintain him and his family in a decent manner.

How is he to get by? Separately, his side job is not enough to maintain him and his compensation is not enough. Together, both his side job and compensation can help him pass over the difficult period he is facing.

So, to accept unemployment compensation and to have a side job might be penalized by law, but it is not stealing.

Greed

In answering Timothy's doubts by saying that he has not stolen in the areas of work, health plans, insurances, paying taxes, and unemployment compensation, Timothy's easygoing side is delighted. It is just what he wanted to hear.

However, Timothy's worrying side is not satisfied. Either the answers do not seem right because he was taught or led to believe differently or they are not right for him because he was not going to do anything about these matters if he had been told he must. So, either way he cannot accept the answers. He is still worried.

Although Timothy's worrying side is wrong in not accepting the answers that he has not stolen, this side of him is right in making the point that Timothy cannot only accept easygoing answers. There are times when he will have to do what is hard because it is the *right* thing to do.

Likewise, Timothy's worrying side is right in the sense that Timothy tends to be greedy. He wants to grab, and even steal, if he can get away with it before men and God. He knows this tendency inside himself and it does need constant watching; still it does not change the picture or the answers we have given.

So

So, Timothy has not stolen. He does need to mature and let his "I" take control over him, not his greed or easygoing side. His worrying about having stolen is not going to help him get "I" control. His whole attention will be on his worries and not on himself and working toward such control.

If, like Timothy, you are troubled in this area of stealing, talk it over with your counselor and listen to what he has to say. Try to hear his voice above the voices of your easygoing side and your worrying side. You do not want *easy* or *hard* answers. You want the *right* answers.

We will consider this area of stealing a bit more in Chapter Twelve. In the meantime, in regard to the cases considered in this chapter, it would be wise for you to adjust your thinking and realize that you have not stolen. It would also be wise to realize the need you have to keep your greed under control.

CHAPTER 10
Confessing Sins

The idea of confessing your sins is not just an idea of the Catholic Church, rather it is an idea that goes all the way back to childhood.

Your parents and others worried over you that you might not grow up right so they trained you and scolded you into doing what they thought was right. They wanted you to be honest with them and tell them when you went against their rules. After you *confessed, were corrected,* and perhaps *punished* to make up for what you had done and to impress on you not to do it again, they felt better, and, in a strange way, you felt better. Rightly or wrongly, everyone felt you were back on the right road.

The Catholic Idea

So, although many think that a confessing of sins is an invention of the Catholic Church, it really is not. Other religions have practiced confession and even modern therapy groups find it helpful.

What is the product of the Catholic Church is the *way* Confession takes place and the *results* it produces.

One, the confessing to an approved priest as the official minister of the Church is Catholic.

Two, the making of a detailed confession of sins — when this is not too inconvenient — is Catholic.

Three, the certainty that one's sins have been forgiven forever is Catholic.

Four, the benefits of being helped not only in regard to the pressures of guilt but also in a special, sacramental way is Catholic.

Thus, the Catholic Church idea of confessing is similar but different from other ideas of confessing. More important, it might even be different from your ideas. If your ideas are different, then you should attempt to change them. To say, "But that is the way I thought it had to be done," is not valid. If you are putting more demands on yourself than the Church does, then your demands have to change.

So, regardless what your worrying side says — and regardless how much your easygoing side rejoices over having things made easier — *you* must attempt to adjust your way of thinking to what is really expected of you. It is not left up to your worrying side to decide in this matter.

Making a Detailed Confession

A big stumbling block for many in confessing is to tell their sins exactly.

There are several reasons for this difficulty.

First, there is a great amount of embarrassment connected with certain sins, especially sins of sex. To admit such sins to one's self and to tell them to another is hard. For some, as with our example of Ann in Chapter Two of this book, it seems impossible to reveal something so shameful. Ann is so embarrassed over what she has done that she wants to run from it and forget it forever. She feels that others would not accept her once they knew.

Second, if a person has been away from Confession for a long time, there is the difficulty of trying to remember the exact number of mortal sins that have been committed.

Embarrassment

Even though the confessor's lips are sealed, it is difficult for everyone — and especially for you — to confess shameful sins. Somehow the picture you want to have of yourself as being innocent and good is disfigured with ugly, embarrassing scars. You want in the worst way to hide those scars.

This is most understandable.

It is also most regrettable. That we are so motivated by a fear of what people will think of us and not by right and wrong is sad.

It is especially sad should such a fear rob you of the full benefits of Confession. The priest has heard countless confessions of weakness and shame. Yours is scarcely different. Surely you can find an understanding priest somewhere who can put you at ease enough so that you can acknowledge what you have done or been.

But is your problem so much a fear of telling someone else what you have done or of telling yourself? If you can accept what you have been, then it is not that difficult to face someone else.

In any event, regardless of why you are afraid, it is worth your while to acknowledge and bring such hidden guilt to the light of day. While it festers inside of you, it is poison. When it is exposed, it can begin to be eliminated and the healing process can begin.

Remembering Sins

In confessing, you should account for all your serious sins and the number of times you committed each.

If you do not remember a kind of sin or the exact number of a particular kind of sin, then a general statement will do. "I think I committed such a sin a number of times. For these and all the sins I have committed, I ask God's pardon."

As far as going into detail with any particular kind of sin, it is better to keep it general. If the confessor wants more information, he will ask you.

That is simple enough. But knowing yourself and the control your worrying side has over you, it is not going to work out that easily. You will find difficulties somewhere.

Perhaps your greatest problem will be over sins you forgot to tell or are not sure you told; or maybe you think you told them incorrectly. What are you to do?

If you have forgotten some sins — especially if you have not been to Confession for a number of years — then wait until your next Confession and mention them *briefly* at that time. But, if you find yourself repeating sins just to be sure, then force yourself not to tell them.

If you find yourself correcting your past confession of sins because you are afraid you did not make them accurately, allow yourself one attempt to correct the matter. If that does not satisfy you, then drop it. It is not worth all the upsetment it is causing. Just make a general statement of sorrow over everything. "Lord, I am sorry, or at least I am trying to be sorry, for all my sins." That is sufficient.

Perhaps the best thing you can do is to come

to some kind of agreement with your confessor on how to handle such matters.

Not an Internal Revenue Agent

Regardless of how exact your worrying side wants you to be in confessing, remember that God is God. He is not an internal revenue agent looking to discover how you have cheated or withheld information.

You may be that way, or others may be that way, but God is not that way.

God's main concern in having you make an exact confession is to have you *stop* and *think* of what you have done so that you can be more aware of your sins and your need for forgiveness. It is hoped that being made more aware you will make some corrections in your life.

Such an examination of conscience was not meant to be a mental torture.

If, for any reason, you are making your examination such a torture, then try to drop the whole thing and simply say the prayer of the Publican in the Gospel, "Lord, be merciful to me a sinner."

"But," you will object, "that is too easy. It should be made harder so that my easygoing side will not get the wrong idea that sins are easily forgiven and that I do not have to worry about committing them."

Your easygoing side will tempt you to look on sin that way, but you do not have to follow its lead.

How Often?

If you are drowning in your worries over

sins, you will want to reach out to your confessor for constant help. This should not be allowed. To be allowed to reach out so freely puts no restriction on your worries. It accomplishes nothing, except to exhaust yourself and your confessor. Actually, if possible, your worries should be handled in private conferences outside of confession time.

So, how often should you confess?

At most, you should not confess more than once a month. Depending on your condition, you might extend that time to once every three months or every six months.

What are you to do with all the sins you might have collected in the meantime?

You simply make an act of love of God, "My God I love you," and those sins are forgiven. Later, when you go to confession at the time fixed by you and your confessor, your act of love becomes a sacrament.

How about receiving Holy Communion without confessing?

You should go as often as you want to, without being forced or restricted.

So

Ann has to face up to her embarrassment. This will not be easy. She has so magnified and made monsters of her feelings of shame that she will try to talk herself out of facing them. This is where an understanding counselor can help. Gently and having won her confidence, he can help her let those monsters out. Surprisingly, once she starts to talk about her feelings of shame, they stop being monsters. They become realities that need facing. She has done something wrong and she must confess it with sorrow. Nothing more is required.

The same applies to you if confessing is a problem for you.

So, for Ann, yourself, and everyone, Confession is not good for the soul if it is abused. God meant it as an act of mercy, not worry. To turn confession time into a torture experience is an abuse. Try not to do it. Try to accept God's mercy, regardless of how much your worrying side opposes it. Once you have received absolution, try not to look back. You have already wasted too much of yourself worrying about your past life.

CHAPTER 11

Promising Amendment

For some, the most difficult part of being forgiven is not the telling of sins and being sorry for them, rather, it is the part of promising to do better. If they did not have to make this promise, it would be so much easier. But they have been told that this promise is necessary to prove the sincerity of their sorrow. And, somehow they themselves realize that rushing out and committing the same sins does not make their sorrow look very good.

So, some promise of amendment is necessary for forgiveness.

How Firm a Promise?

The firmness of the promise of amendment people feel they must make depends on whether their easygoing side or their worrying side is in control of them.

If their easygoing side is in control, then they do not feel that they have to be that definite or sure of their promise of amendment. They can be satisfied with their words at the time of Confession that they will try to do better. A half hour later they might change their minds, but at least at the time of Confession they have convinced themselves they will try.

If their worrying side has completely taken over, then words of promising amendment are not enough. They can almost hear their parents or teachers who trained them say, "Good intentions are not good enough. The road to hell is paved with good intentions. You need evidence, facts, to back up your words. So, if you did not keep your promise, you were not sincere. You were only playing games with yourself and God. If you do not back up your promise with actions, your promise is no good.''

This proving of their sincerity becomes an impossible problem for people whose worrying side has taken over. They are almost certain they will commit those sins again, so how can they feel confident or sincere about their promise to try not to?

This taking over of his worrying side is Michael's problem in Chapter Two of this book. Perhaps it is also your problem.

Some kind of middle position based on you as a person must be found.

A Realistic Position

The task of changing your ways is real work. It is not the result of daydreams, nor should it be the result of fear.

Your easygoing side would daydream you into believing that you can change easily.

Your worrying side would hold the gun of fear at your head, demanding an immediate, complete change, or else.

Neither kind of change is realistic or lasting.

The promise to do better that is needed for a forgiveness of sins cannot be that firm. It is a realization that a change is needed in your life and that you are going to try to take the first steps toward that change. The final product of a complete change will have to wait.

As you saw in Chapter Six that a developing of "I" control must begin with little things, the same is true of your promise of amendment. If you are yielding to sexual sins because you immediately give in to your impulses for pleasure, then try to slow yourself down a bit to consider what you are about to do. That might help.

A further step might be to occasionally discipline yourself in areas of pleasure that are not sinful. This could help break you of the habit of immediately giving into your pleasure impulses. It would also help you feel more sincere about your desires and efforts to change.

As Applied to Michael

So, despite what his easygoing side would like to believe he can do or his worrying side insists he must do, Michael must convince himself that he is not capable of quickly, perfectly amending his life.

Michael is Michael.

He is not one of the saints who had a giant conversion and completely changed. That would be a miracle. Such miracles are rare.

On the other hand, Michael can begin to try to change. He can try to be sincere about his desire to change. Playing games or pretending to want to change so as to feel forgiven is not going to help Michael change or grow up.

So Michael should not worry himself sick trying to feel that he has a firm purpose of amendment. He simply is not capable of such a firm purpose of amendment. That will come as he grows from within himself. God is patient and generous and will accept whatever Michael has to offer at this time.

To ask more of Michael is unrealistic and

would be doomed to failure. He simply is not capable of that much more. So to force or frighten him into giving what he does not have is not going to work. His failure to live up to so high a standard would only push him into frustration and despair. He would end up doing nothing.

As Applied to You

If you are worried about being forgiven because you do not feel you can amend your life, then ask yourself some realistic questions.

Do you see a need to change?

Do you want to try to change?

Can you find someone to help you change?

If you, not just your worrying side, see a need for a change and you are willing to try to change, then be satisfied with your promise of amendment. Do not waste time or energy trying to convince yourself how sincere or insincere your promise of amendment is. Use that time and energy on actually setting about to change.

CHAPTER 12

Putting It Together

As if working with a jigsaw puzzle, we have been turning over and gathering together the pieces that make up your scrupulous condition.

Now it is time to try to put it all together.

Obviously, this is not an easy task.

To make our task a little easier, we will divide our consideration into four parts. First, we must make it absolutely clear that your main problem is *panic*. Second, because you cannot deal directly with panic, you may need some necessary shortcuts to be freed of obligations arising from the past. Third, you need an escape hatch to free yourself as soon as your panic threatens. Fourth, we will consider some of the positive things you can do to help yourself.

First

Regardless of *how* you became so, you are scrupulous because you have stirred up and released an inner fear or panic that has taken over control of you. The hurt this panic causes you is so painful that you would do anything to be rid of it or keep it away from you. This is why you cling so stubbornly to your overcautious ways and are willing to repeat your actions until they are perfectly safe.

So, panic is the main problem.

All your doubts, all your feelings of sex, of harming others, or of stealing, all your past sins and fears of sinning again — all of these problems have become unbearable because they stir up your panic.

They press a "panic" button inside your nerves and your worrying side takes over control. It tortures you with doubts until the panic goes away or at least lets up. Perhaps only you know how terrible this torture can be.

When you are in this state of panic, nothing brings relief. Certainly, arguing with your worrying side is not the answer. It only makes your panic worse.

You have tried to work out some ways to deal with your panic — to keep it from happening or to get rid of it as soon as it happens. Thus, you try to "undo" an action or you try to keep away from anything that might trigger off your panic. Your ways help a little, but the cost you have to pay of being so totally exact in what you say or do or of looking ridiculous to others is too high a price to pay.

You need a better way to handle your panic.

The better way is the way of "knowing" what is really expected of you and to develop your "I" power to keep your worrying side under control.

But knowing and gaining "I" control take time and are good to work toward, but they are not going to stop the panic that is torturing you right here and now. You need some temporary relief to cope with now.

Second

A start toward getting some here and now relief is to try to eliminate some of the things that are upsetting you from your past life. To do this, you will need to take some "shortcuts."

Thus, if you have lived a life of sexual abuse, you are not going to be able to account and be sorry for all of it individually or in detail. At best, you are only going to be able to confess what stands out the most. That is sufficient. To torture yourself or your confessor with attempts to reexamine or repeat sins is not only not necessary; it is harmful.

If you have stolen or secretly owe a large sum of money and it would be too frightening or too difficult to repay it, then you are not going to be able to pay it back.

If you have harmed someone by an abortion or lack of proper attention, you are not going to be able to undo the harm that has been done.

If for these or countless other reasons you are paralyzed in your thinking or acting, it is better for you and society to wipe away the debt and start fresh, and never have to worry or go back over it again.

Your confessor or counselor can help you to determine the shortcuts you need to give yourself a fresh start.

Third

But the biggest problem of all is to slow down your panic over the things that are happening now.

Perhaps a doctor's prescription of some calming tranquilizers will help.

But, on your part, you are going to have to try to help yourself. You desperately need a ready "escape" hatch to free you as soon as you become aware that you are panicking.

In the past, "blind obedience" to your confessor was proposed as a kind of escape hatch. As a matter of fact, it has helped some, but not too many. It is asking a great deal of a panicking person to entrust his safety to someone else.

What other kinds of escape hatches are there?

The best escape hatch of all is the truth.

The truth is that if your panic can have so much control over you, it is doubtful that you have enough control over your feelings to be *fully* responsible for your actions.

Obviously, you have some control over your actions, but not enough to assume a full blame for them. In many ways, you are in a condition like that of a child. You *know* certain things are wrong and you *know* you are doing those wrong things, but you do not have enough control or maturity to be fully accountable.

So, the first truth or escape hatch is to recognize that because of your condition you are not fully responsible for your actions. You have not committed a serious sin.

Thus, when your worrying side accuses you of having committed a serious sin, you can answer, "I have not" or "Not guilty."

The second truth or escape hatch is not to argue with your worrying side. To argue is only going to stir up your panic. So, as soon as your worrying side begins to accuse you of serious sin or as soon as you begin to feel anxious, force yourself not to argue with your worrying side. Simply tell yourself, "Do not argue." Then try to get busy doing something that will occupy your attention.

If you can accept and immediately apply these two escape hatches of "NOT GUILTY" and "DO NOT ARGUE," then you can control the panic before it can get control over you.

By Whose Authority?

"But," you might object, "how can I accept these truths of not being guilty and of not arguing with my worrying side? I *feel* I must argue with my worrying side to convince myself that I am not guilty; otherwise I feel I am."

You can either accept these truths because you see for yourself that they are true or you can accept them on my authority as a Doctor in Moral Guidance.

This might seem like "blind obedience" where you are doing something because a confessor has ordered you to obey, but it is not. On the contrary, this is an acceptance of truth because of another's learning and because you have made his learning your own. Thus, when you act, it is your action — not something your confessor ordered.

In using me and this book as the authority for *your* decision to accept these escape hatches, you are doing what you do in other areas of life. You use teachers, doctors, and other professional people as the authority for many of your decisions because they have specialized in their field of learning. The same is true in the area of scruples. Obviously, my long years of study and experience with scruples make me a specialist. So, to use me as an authority should not be that difficult.

"But," you object, "these escape hatches would give my carefree, easygoing side the go ahead to do anything it wants and not feel guilty. Surely, you do not want that to happen?''

Applying Brakes

To calm your fears about the takeover of your easygoing side, it might be better to restrict these escape hatches to only "head" actions of thoughts, feelings, and desires and to actions where you "fear" you might have done something wrong.

Thus, you would only accuse yourself of sin if you actually stole someone else's money, actually killed or struck a blow at someone, or committed a deliberate, external act of masturbation or a complete act of sex with someone who is not a marriage partner.

In any other area of thoughts, feelings, and desires or in dealing with fears of having harmed or wished someone over to evil or in acts of sex that happen upon awakening or are the results of thoughts and imagination, then apply the escape hatches — NOT GUILTY, DO NOT ARGUE.

Hopefully, this will give you and your counselor a tool to eventually break the hold your panic and worrying side have over you.

Keeping Busy

As we have already indicated, besides these escape hatches of NOT GUILTY, DO NOT ARGUE, it would be wise to always have something handy to occupy your mind. Your worrying side is not going to let up on its own. You need to take your thoughts and attention away from it. The best way to do this is to have something else to think about and occupy your attention.

It would be better if the distraction were something external like going for a walk, doing some work, or some other physical activity. This would serve both purposes of distracting you and of helping to relieve your body of some of the "worry" tension and energy it has built up.

You probably will not *feel* like doing anything external. In fact, you would probably prefer to hide in sleep and hope that when you wake up it will all have been a bad dream. That is understandable, still it would be good to force yourself to at least try something. To lie idly around gives your worrying side the whole stage of your attention.

The practical things you can do to keep busy can be worked out with your counselor.

Being Honest

Before you can really accept these escape hatches of NOT GUILTY, DO NOT ARGUE with the accusations of your worrying side, you will have to be honest with yourself about your condition.

Although you might have a very fine intellect and talents beyond measure, they are not helping you because you are not in control of yourself. Your feelings are. Because they are running you, your feelings have you only concerned with getting pleasures and avoiding displeasures or pain. It might hurt to realize this, but it is true. When panic strikes, you have about as much control and responsibility as a terrified child. You *need* the escape hatches of NOT GUILTY, DO NOT ARGUE.

So, your first step is to accept the truth of your condition. You simply are not in a position to be responsible for the sinfulness of your "head" actions of thoughts, feelings, and desires nor of past actions involving obligations nor of sins you fear you might have committed.

Following closely on this acceptance of your condition is the realization that God has accepted your condition and will not hold you any more responsible than your condition allows.

It is now up to *you* to immediately apply these escape hatches to your panic so that you can eventually learn to live a normal, responsible life.

Fourth

Once you have accepted your condition and have taken the necessary shortcuts to free yourself of past obligations and are quick to use your escape hatches to fight your panic, then you are in a position to learn some better ways to handle life.

Without realizing it, you have used panic in two ways: either to get you to do things you would otherwise avoid or postpone facing; or to run away from things because you did not feel you could handle them perfectly enough to satisfy your worrying side. In this latter case, your cry has been, "I can't handle my 'bad' feelings or temptations or make decisions on my own. Someone has to help me and reassure me that everything is alright."

That has been a legitimate cry, but now, being freed of past obligations and of so many difficulties that could press your "panic" button, you are in a position to get on with living.

Your first efforts should be to try to accept your humanity with its sexual drive, anger feelings, greedy desires, etc. Stop running away from them as if they should not exist. They are a part of you. They do not have to steal control away from you. God and nature have given you an ego or "I" to unite you and be in control of yourself.

From now on, it is this "I" control that is to be stressed, not whether you have committed sin or not. Did you or did you not lose "I" control over yourself? Did you let a part of you take over control? If you did, what are *you* going to do to get back control?

Later on, when you have developed as a person, as an "I," you and your counselor can begin to hold you accountable when you allow your parts to win control and violate your own good order and God's good order. For now, your efforts should be totally directed toward being aware of yourself as a person or "I."

CHAPTER 13

A Belief in Love

Having considered some ways of acting that can help you deal with your scrupulous condition, we do not want to overlook the most important element of all — love.

It is only a belief in love, especially God's love, that can help you understand and accept the shortcuts and escape hatches you need to fight off panic.

If you have loved or been loved, you know how generous and forgiving love can be. If you have not loved or been loved, you find generosity and forgiveness too hard to believe.

Two Different Ways

There are two ways to approach life and God.

There is the inferior way of justice and the superior way of love. This needs explaining.

The way of justice is the way where everything is measured out exactly. You give what you receive and you receive what you give — no more, no less. It is the way of an eye for an eye and a tooth for a tooth.

Thus, if you have offended God or your fellow-man in a particular way, then you must make up for that offense in the same way or in some way that is equal to the offense. Each and every offense must be accounted for and settled. There is no question of "shortcuts" or "escape hatches." You either pay totally or you are punished.

The way of love is careful not to offend but it is full of mercy if you should. You give and get lovingly, not miserly.

Thus, if you have offended God or your

fellow-man and they are loving enough to forgive and cancel out your offense, the offense is canceled. They expect no more, except perhaps that you are sorry and will try not to commit the offense again. And, surprisingly, they really want you to be sorry and try to improve for your own sake, rather than theirs.

Such are the ways of justice and love. It would seem that, when it is possible, love's ways are to be preferred.

Neither, Nor

So love's ways are not the extremely cautious ways of your worrying side. These would be more the ways of justice.

On the other hand, love's ways are not the careless, irresponsible ways of your easygoing side. That would be too childish.

Somewhere in between these two extremes love finds her nest. Love can be both exacting and forgiving, depending on circumstances. If you are trying now to do what is right, love is exacting, without going overboard. If you have tried and failed, love is forgiving, without condoning or excusing the wrong you have done.

All that love asks is that you do what you can at this moment. The past is over and the future has not yet come. You only have this moment to love and try to live up to love's expectations. If you try and fail, or if you fail because you have not tried, you can still try again — now.

Love would not want you to brood over the past or make big promises for the future. These are more the ways of justice.

No, love is satisfied with what you have to offer this very moment. Do now what you would have liked to have done or what you promise to do. Do it now as best you can. It might not come out perfectly, but that is alright. Love is satisfied that you did something.

A Belief in Love

But what if you do not feel you have ever really experienced love? You have neither loved others so generously or so forgivingly nor been loved by others in these ways. What are you to do to convince yourself that such love exists and that it exists for you?

This is a difficult question to answer.

Most people you know do not love so generously and in such a forgiving manner. In fact, they are pretty self-centered in their loving. They want a return for what they give and they have a limit to how much they will give or put up with. If anything, they, too, are looking for such a generous, forgiving love from others. It would seem that everyone is looking, but few are finding or are able to give such a love.

And yet, such a love does exist. Certainly God has shown this kind of love; otherwise why would he have done all that he did? It would make no sense. Were not Christ's dying words, "Forgive them, Father . . ."?

So, such a love does exist, at least with God.

"But," you object, "I do not *feel* that such a generous, forgiving love exists for me. It would be just my luck that God's generosity and forgiveness will have been all used up when my time for judgment comes. All he will have left is his justice. I cannot take such a chance.''

Obviously, your feelings are too frightened to realize that God cannot be that way. God is not like a limited human parent, teacher, or judge. He just is not.

But, no matter how you feel because you have never personally seen or felt such a love, at least you can *believe* that such a love exists in God. Belief is that way. You do not necessarily experience what you believe, but you have enough evidence to go on to believe that a thing is true.

This certainly is true with God. You can believe in his generous, forgiving love.

Therefore Try . . .

So, on the basis of a belief in God's love, try your hardest to accept the shortcuts you and your counselor feel are necessary to cancel out your past debts.

Try to apply *immediately* the escape hatches of NOT GUILTY, DO NOT ARGUE when panic strikes.

Try to accept your humanity with its variety of impulses and feelings.

Try to accept God's mercy in your behalf.

Try to develop your "I" power so that you — not your easygoing side or your worrying side — control you.

In a word, try *to believe* in love.

CHAPTER 14

Some Words
of Encouragement

To this point, we have considered what could be a help for overcoming your scrupulous condition.

It has been like standing on the shore and tossing out a rope to you who are out in the deep water — drowning.

Hopefully you can reach out to the words of this book and hopefully they can help bring you back safely to the shore. It may take some doing, but it can be done because the ideas of this book are sound and have helped others.

In the meantime, until relief comes, try not to be too discouraged by your lack of success. Your efforts, although not immediately successful, will succeed. Besides, regardless of their outcome, they have a special value with God.

Understanding God

Obviously, God does not want you to be suffering so.

God meant religion to be "good news," not bad news. However, that is what religion has become for you. The good news has soured into bad news.

Whose fault is this?

It is hard to say.

Your background training has a lot to say about your present condition. Your training could have been too severe or too lax. In neither case would you be properly prepared for life. If you see everything through worrying eyes, you will worry about almost everything. If you see everything through carefree, easygoing eyes, you will be setting yourself up for a day of reckoning. Neither way of viewing life is balanced enough to give you any kind of normal stability.

Is God to blame for your condition? Why has he allowed this to happen? Why does he not do something about it? Does he like to see you suffer so? Surely, he could do something to help you. Why doesn't he?

These are difficult questions to answer, and really you do not want answers to questions. You want relief.

But relief does not just happen. You have to work for it by straightening things out; otherwise you would be right back into the situation all over again and would not have learned anything or grown up.

There are good reasons why God has allowed you to arrive at this condition, and they are not just negative, childish reasons of being punished for your sins. What exactly these reasons are is not known. You will probably have to wait to discover and appreciate them at a later time. In the meantime, if you understand God at all, you know his reasons are good ones.

A Crown of Thorns

So, regardless of how or why you have arrived at this point of torture, you are like someone wearing a crown of thorns on his head. You can hardly think a thought without the thorns pressing in on you. The fears and doubts that pressure your brain and being can be the most terrible known to man.

You are too frightened to give up.

You are too confused to fight.

You are not perfect enough to please and settle the guilt of your worrying side.

You cannot relax or let up because you are too afraid that your easygoing side will sneak in and take control.

You are relatively healthy of body but you feel more crippled than someone physically handicapped.

You try praying but that does not seem to help.

You run for help to confessors, doctors, and even therapists, but they only help a little and for the moment.

You want to cry, complain, scream, and kick but that will not help.

In a few words, you are in a real agony and you do not know what to do.

An Acceptable Crucifixion

Without trying to glorify or encourage your sufferings, you can reassure yourself that what you are enduring can be offered to God.

"But I feel that my sufferings are all coming from some form of guilt. Besides, I do not accept what I am suffering. So how can I offer such sufferings to God?"

It does not matter. Your sufferings still count and can be offered to God out of whatever little love and trust you have in him. You do not understand, but you are trying to love and trust God. It is that love and trust that continues to exist, despite your sufferings, that are acceptable.

As in the Gospel story of the widow putting her tiny coin into the collection box, you are giving from what you barely have, and that is what counts. The widow was credited as having given more than the rest who put in big coins out of their abundance. She put in from her very need and was praised.

No one is scraping the bottom of the barrel more than you. You are being crucified by your guilt and excessive need to be overcautious and make everything perfect. Trying to love and trust under those conditions — even if only out of fear — you are actually being heroic.

And that is acceptable to God. Your cry is like the cry of Christ on the Cross, "My God, my God, why have you forsaken me?"

Add to that cry, as best you can, "Father, into your hands I entrust myself," and strangely enough your suffering becomes something like that of Christ.

In Conclusion

So, although your condition is an unhealthy one and should be remedied as soon as possible, the efforts you are making and the suffering you are going through can have a value. Give them to God with whatever love and trust you have and realize that your offering is acceptable.

It is bad enough that you are suffering so. Why waste it? Strangely enough, although this truth does not take away the darkness that surrounds you, it can be a star in the pitch-black night that makes the darkness a little less bitter and scary.

For further help, here are two other volumes from Liguori Publications:

How to Understand and Overcome Depression
by Earnest Larsen

A hopeful, helpful book for anyone who has ever fought depression or who is struggling with depression now. The author, Earnest Larsen, speaks the language of sympathy and concern. Hand in hand with the reader, Larsen walks up five steps — steps to find acceptance of yourself, of others, and of God. Larsen gives his readers help in finding these open doors in the walls of depression. **$3.95**

How to Develop a Better Self-Image
by Russell M. Abata, C.SS.R., S.T.D.

A beautiful ''self-help'' book that should lead to self-discovery, self-control, and a greater acceptance of self, others, and God. The author discusses: the person your *training* wants you to be, the person your *feelings* want you to be, and the person God *designed you to become*. Blends practical psychology with a Christian view of life. **$3.95**

Order from your local bookstore or write to:
Liguori Publications, Box 060, Liguori, Missouri 63057-9999
*(Please add $1.00 for postage and handling for
orders under $5.00; $1.50 for orders over $5.00.)*